For Je

Jay

The Zen of Financial Peril

The Art of Happiness in Crisis

JAY G. M. TAFFET

The Zen of Financial Peril

The Art of Happiness in Crisis

JAY G. M. TAFFET

The Zen of Financial Peril
The Art of Happiness in Crisis
by Jay G. M. Taffet

ISBN: 978-0-615-38570-9

Library of Congress Control Number: 2010935292

Book Design by Lydia Inglett Ltd.
www.lydiainglett.com
PRINTED IN THE UNITED STATES OF AMERICA

Published by

Steven L. Morris Publishing
P.O. Box 230153
Montgomery, Alabama 36123

www.zenoffinancialperil.com

For my readers.

It was the power of the transforming themes
you'll experience in this book that compelled me
to write it so I could share them with you.
I hope you find the same sense of self-empowerment
and spiritual faith that I did.
And, of course, the amazing proof.

Contents

CHAPTER 1

Recognizing our Personal Evolution

Have you ever thought how easy and fulfilling life would be if you could identify the moment when your life actually evolved?

Imagine that you find yourself in circumstances that seem challenging and exhausting, but you have the ability and insight to realize that you are at the precipice of great opportunity, the summit over which you can clearly see the next phase of your life. You don't see things as bad. There are no issues which paralyze you, and you don't dwell on what has occurred and what could happen in the future. You accept your life as it is and you don't have any anxiety about where it may go. You feel completely empowered by where you are and what you may do next.

Four years ago, I could not do any of this. I was plagued by the past and anxious about the future. I felt as if life was a wave pool that was sometimes calm enough to float in and enjoy, but, other times, a challenge to even tread water.

The conditions of my life seemed to be erratic and my actions and perspectives were just by-products of the chance that was my existence.

Everything seemed to be luck and, even when my efforts were well invested in an ambition or action, I still did not feel responsible for the outcome.

Of course, I felt successful at times, but each success was just a way-station for the next stumble or, worse, failure.

Thus, it made no sense to set before me two great ambitions and especially not together: an entrepreneurial business goal and a complete self- transformation.

Four years ago, I decided to quit my career and pursue a business venture that was a moonshot if it were to succeed.

I was going to build my own brand of aviation facilities at airports with the most complex bureaucracies and a bulwark of regulations that made winning approval to do what I endeavored a near impossibility. And I was going to attempt to do this in an investment environment that was already receding, especially in the narrow industry I'd chosen.

None of these variables mattered to me because I had a desire to construct a professional path that would be the ultimate confluence of my aviation background and my real estate development profession.

And, to make the venture even more perilous, I was going to do this by investing everything I had in terms of cash, assets and ability to borrow. I was going to take the ultimate entrepreneurial leap of faith, and I was going to do it alone.

At the same time, I launched the biggest self-transformation process that one can take in life. I was going to examine every inch of my past and every contour of my future and find a different place in life where I felt more in control and more empowered to make life happen as I desired.

My goal was to evaluate my personal identity, religious affiliation, political perspectives, cultural ambitions, social roles, relationships with friends and family, the contents of my home, the photos in my albums, the clothes in my closet, the things I put in my pocket...absolutely everything that comprised my life mentally, emotionally, physically and spiritually. I would leave nothing untouched and unexamined.

If there was an object in my space or a thought in my head, it was going to be evaluated. And I was determined to do this as honestly and thoroughly as it could be done.

I was intent on becoming the observer of my life so I could determine the kind of life I truly desired.

My paths were set. I was constructing a

professional path that was lined with risk and potential loss, and I was transforming my life through a massive house cleaning of everything that defined me.

At the time, I was not fully conscious of why I would want to take on both projects simultaneously, but it just felt right to do it. I was scared on both fronts, and my anxiety could not have been higher when I made my move.

In one week, I quit my job, launched my venture and inventoried my physical and mental space to see what would stay and what would go.

Each process was painful, and the sense of loss I felt was incredibly consuming. I felt completing my journey would be near impossible, and my desire to quit and return to stable and familiar ground was very compelling.

The thought I had made a terrible mistake was drenching me with anxiety and regret. All I wanted was to return to a calm shore where my personal risk was minimized and my life was not deconstructed.

And then it became clear.

This book is about the clarity and insight that rooted in me when I looked within for the courage and determination to take the reins of my life and set out on a transforming journey. It is about understanding how our thoughts shape our lives and how to mine the resources in our world to make a life that reflects our true desires.

My goal is to share with you the tools that will transform the seemingly complex world of mysticism and spirituality into practical and simple exercises that will empower you with a sense of control and purpose.

I will show you over the next six chapters that you are the captain of your own ship, and that every detail of your past and future are exactly what you planned.

And I will show you that uncertainty is the garden of opportunity and the foundation for success because realizing a goal is not the goal. The faith and constitution to set the goal and pursue it is the goal.

Success is not what we envision when we start a journey because we can't predict all the hues and shapes that will make it a success.

Success is investing yourself in a journey that will take you to a shore more enriching than where you are now.

There you will find another world of more abundant success than you could have ever described in a business or personal plan.

I should know, because four years later I find myself on the verge of financial peril, with the business on the cusp of launching after years of setbacks and turns I could not have predicted, but I've never been happier.

My journey has been successful because I find myself exactly where I desired to be, on the summit of self-awareness and business opportunity.

Despite the financial pressure of my existence today, I have no doubt that I will be successful and that my life will be enriched. And I'm convinced of this even if the business venture does not assume the success picture I painted for it years ago.

My faith and perseverance and my understanding of desire and how it manifests in our lives is my success because these are the variables that will take me to the shore. I finally trust my ability to navigate my own ship and to find the right current that will deliver me to my destination, whether that destination be the one I saw first or the one I see now.

I can finally see the precise moment when my life will evolve.

CHAPTER 2

The Separation of Mind and Soul

WE BEGIN OUR JOURNEY into taking control of our lives with an understanding of the contrasting functions of the mind and soul.

The mind and soul are two very different parts of us. Our thoughts and feelings emanate from the mind and define who we are intellectually, socially and emotionally.

We spend a lifetime learning, assessing, storing and retrieving from our mind, and we come to rely on its ability to understand and evaluate the world around us. The process is so natural that we come to trust the mind to do this without conscious effort. In a sense, we are defined by our mind and its functions because everything we think and communicate comes from it.

And that's where the danger begins.

Our mind is a tool we use to survive in the world. It analyzes an infinite amount of data and stimuli every second to help us function, and it performs these calculations at speeds that we cannot comprehend.

Thus, we do not try to intervene in the process of our thinking because we cannot keep up with its powerful functioning. This hands-off relationship with our mind allows it to generate thoughts, memories and predictions uncensored and ungoverned which often leads to feelings and emotions that are also equally ungoverned. The result is often fear, anxiety, regret, sadness and suffering.

We can be living normally and happily and, all of the sudden, there is an overwhelming sensation of dread that consumes us because of a thought or feeling that pops into our mind.

We may recognize the context or association that put the thought or feeling there, but we are still a victim of its presence, seemingly powerless to eradicate it.

Imagine if we reversed the tables and actually took the driver seat where the mind's functions are concerned, continually monitoring what it generates so we aren't surprised by what it gives us. It will still naturally give us the same volatile thoughts and feelings, and we still might not know where they came from, but now, since we are watching, we can quickly recover from a disturbing thought or feeling that does not apply to our lives.

Put another way, any thought or feeling that causes suffering typically deals with the past or the future. It rarely has to do with what's happening right now. It may seem sometimes that you are dreading what's happening right now, but it really is a "what if" assessment you are making of what's happening at that moment. It's a "if this happens this way, it will be bad" perspective you are taking. It's anxiety about the future and fear about what could come from something happening right now.

On the flip side, if it's not a thought or feeling that is causing fear or anxiety about the future, it's a thought or feeling that is causing regret or pain about the past. It's a trip back in time to a circumstance or situation where you suffered, or thought you suffered, and you feel the emotion again, maybe even more intensely than when it actually happened. It's an overwhelming, sometimes paralyzing, sensation.

However, if we know that these disturbing thoughts and feelings are rooted in the past or the future, then we can become the governor of our mind. We can see the thought begin to form and feel the emotion that it causes and tell our mind that we don't want to participate. We can't stop our mind, but we can separate ourselves from its functioning, observe what it is doing and protect ourselves from the impact of what it generates.

If we can simply side-step the thoughts and feelings that don't apply to us, we can minimize their impact in our lives. We learn that we are the gatekeeper of what we will allow to root in our consciousness, and we begin to experience life with more control and balance.

We are not subject to wild emotional swings anymore because we are governing which emotions we agree to subscribe to. We are choosing when we will constructively revisit the past to mine a lesson or project ourselves into the future to refine a strategy, but we don't spend any time there anymore. We find that past clue or the future glimpse and then we leave. We are not saddled with the emotional weight of regret, anxiety or fear that keeps us there.

We are making conscious decisions about our thoughts and feelings and metering which emotions we want to experience. Our mind continues to function as it should, but we are now the filter through which we experience life...on our terms.

The other component of the mind that is equally disruptive if not monitored is the ego. The ego is a vital component of the mind and the key to our survival.

We rely on our ego to give us the confidence and ability to learn and compete and achieve our goals. We feel empowered by the contributions of our ego and enjoy the pleasure of success because of the self-reliance that it gives us. We need the ego to live and function successfully in this world, and we recognize the power it gives us to accomplish our goals.

But the ego has a lot of problems. It is an unbridled generator of thoughts that ensure our primacy over others and an unregulated spigot of reassurance that we are capable of anything we want to accomplish. The ego does not have boundaries and it does not respond well to any limits that are imposed on it.

Left unchecked, the ego would be more than happy to take the reins of our mind and cultivate an endless and selfish path of indulgence and pleasure without any regard for anybody or anything in its way. War and aggression are the projection of ego as are pride and vanity.

All that we do to ourselves and the world around us that is hurtful and damaging is the work of ego. Sure, all that we achieve in discovery and development in our world can also be the work of the ego, but we can discover and develop without the ego whereas we can't be aggressive or self-inflated without it.

In the same way that we have to watch what our mind generates in terms of disruptive thoughts and feelings, we have to continually watch our ego and what it is trying to accomplish.

The ego is consumed with ambition and self-importance and it needs to make the biggest splash it can to be noticed and congratulated for its achievements.

In the same way that we have to filter the positive thoughts and feelings from the disruptive ones, we have to separate the positive and goal-oriented actions of the ego from the negative and self-serving ones that lead to aggression, vanity and misplaced pride.

We have to learn to watch the ego and recognize when it switches from positive to negative influence and consciously reject the input that will potentially lead to disruption or discord.

Just like with the thoughts and feelings that make us experience regret, anxiety and fear, we have to know that if we feel insulted, violent or self-inflated, it's because the ego has taken over and is telling our mind to react negatively in the present situation.

We have to know that we can see the ego influence in our mind and that we have the ability to prevent the result - to *not feel* insulted and violent or superior and self-inflated.

We can choose to let the insult linger without a reaction, to not respond to aggression or catapult ourselves above others, and we can do this without any submission or sublimation of our personality.

Of course, if someone is trying to hurt us physically, we have to defend ourselves, and, if someone is slandering us, we have to respond. But if it's just an empty provocation or irresponsible words, we have a choice about how we respond. We can minimize our ego and calm our mind and decide to allow another part of ourself to formulate our response.

We can allow our soul to feed us the insight and empathy we need to be assertive and constructive, not aggressive and damaging. We can realign the prism of our perception and give the mind and ego a rest while the more important part of ourself addresses the situation with calm and creativity.

THE SOUL

I wrote this book because I wanted to present spirituality and mysticism in a very practical way to illustrate that we all have the innate ability to form and enrich our lives with just a simple change of perspective and understanding.

I wanted to demystify, if you will, the parlance of the spiritual world and bring the concepts to the everyday language of our lives. I've read many books that did this somewhat successfully, but I've not encountered anything that offers proof that spiritual perspective is an exercise we can do everyday, to not just manifest what we desire in our lives, but understand our past with true clarity and comfort.

The next few chapters will get into this practical approach, and I think you will be startled by the simplicity of the concepts and exercises that prove to you that pain and suffering are optional and that a meaningful and enriching life is our purpose.

But, first, to lay the groundwork for this next step, I have to introduce the soul in a way that may seem counterintuitive to both the spiritualist and the religious.

The soul is the purview of the universe. It is not contained in or confined by your body. It is part of everything living and constantly evolving and reshaping itself regardless of any conscious effort or attention you give it.

The soul is your source of energy and insight, your wellspring of compassion and potential. It is not related to your mind, and it is not controlled by your thoughts. All the thoughts, feelings and emotions that you identify with, whether positive or negative, have no connection to your soul or your potential.

There is nothing you can do to impact your

soul with either pain or salvation. You have no control over your soul because you alone do not possess it.

This is a radical concept to read and absorb because we live in a world where we are taught that our mind, body and spirit are the trinity of our existence, and that we are equally responsible for the development and maintenance of all three.

We have naturally defaulted to this understanding because it seems plausible that we are the sum of the mental, physical and spiritual.

But we are not. We are the sum of the mental and the physical. We can develop our mind and exercise its abilities as much or as little as we want.

We can think positive or negative thoughts and we can learn everything that inspires us or choose not to learn anything. We can use our mind for good or bad, and we can employ our mind productively in our lives or live mindlessly.

It is all our choice.

The same goes for our body. We can maintain our body through good physical health – diet and exercise – or we can choose to atrophy. We can develop our physical abilities and become proficient at self-conditioning and competitive exercises or we can choose to remain idle and accept what may deteriorate or destruct in our body.

We have a lifetime to make these choices, and we can change or reverse course whenever we want to by simple intent and action.

But you can't do the same with your soul. It is not part of your choice matrix, and it is not something you can develop or refine. It is already perfect.

Your soul is part of the everything that is the living world, and, even in the most dehumanized and oppressive conditions, your soul cannot be spoiled.

Your soul is eternal, and it is eternally untouched by anything you do, think or intend in your life.

This is the first secret. You have dominion over your mind and body but not your soul. And, if you have no control over your soul, then you always have a perfect, unspoiled resource to draw from for personal development.

You have unlimited access to an infinite well-spring of insight, understanding, wisdom and perspective, the variables you need to live life fully and richly.

Notice that insight, understanding, wisdom and perspective are all nebulous terms that could also connote smartness or intelligence, things we associate with the mind.

They are not the same.

Insight, understanding, wisdom and perspective are soul states, not mental states. These capacities are the resources you need to use the data collected in your mind for healthy and positive purposes.

In other words, you can spend a lifetime learning and mastering every intellectual discipline that defines our world, every science, language and mathematical principle that has and will ever exist, and you still won't have touched the surface of the information that comprises the living world.

Look at it this way: If all the information in the world was viewed as a pie, the information you know you know would be a slice thinner than an atom; the information you know you don't know, maybe the size of an atom; and the information *you don't know you don't know,* the entire pie.

We don't know where insight comes from; we don't know how understanding is mastered; we don't know how we mine wisdom; and we don't know how we attract and employ perspective.

All we know is that these things are worthy ingredients to have in our lives because, without them, we could not fully develop and grow into the best versions of ourselves.

If we know that our soul is the source of all insight, understanding, wisdom and perspective, now we know where to look to find it.

Notice I did not say *search,* just *look,* because your infinite wellspring of information is right there, right in front of you. Both your mind and your soul are right there in front of you.

The only difference is that your mind is making a lot of noise and your soul is still, so you naturally notice the mind. And add to that the fact that the mind desperately wants to be noticed all the time and will resort to anything to get your attention, and you can go a lifetime without ever noticing your soul and what it has to offer.

We identify with the mind and its thoughts and feelings because they are being heaved at us around the clock. We are so busy sifting through these constant deliveries, we don't have the time or the energy to look for other packages. We are content with the free gifts being offered everyday, so there is no reason to go mining for others.

And because the mind is so accessible and bountiful, we don't feel the need to look for other sources of information.

We can go a lifetime not knowing – and content not to know – that there is an unlimited well of information right in front of us that makes the mind look inconsequential.

But here's the twist. You do look into this well all the time and unconsciously draw from it.

Every time you pray, meditate or focus, you are tapping into this source.

You are asking for insight, understanding, wisdom and perspective, just not in a connected, conscious sort of way. You are beseeching a higher power for guidance and direction in a specific part of your life and, whether it be God, Adonai, Allah, The Source, The All, whatever you identify with, you are drawing from the same well. And your soul is part of this well.

The secret is to consciously tap into your soul – to live an engaged life in the physical world, but constantly in a state of prayer, meditation or focus.

If you can take the still, calm moments you reserve for yourself to tap into the wellspring of insight, understanding, wisdom and perspective, you can learn to take *every* moment, regardless of its activity, to do the same thing.

Remember, your mind is working on auto-pilot generating thoughts, assessing data, developing strategy; it does not need you to keep the machine running, so you are free to engage your soul even while living productively and constructively in the world.

You can drive a car and tap into your soul for insight; you can engage in lively conversation while you mine your soul for understanding; you can write a business plan and peer into your soul for wisdom; and you can play tennis and consult your soul for perspective.

You achieve perfect duality of mind/body and soul once you realize you have unlimited, eternal access to your soul and all the perfect information it contains.

You function in the world, tending to your responsibilities, but you are perpetually immersed in insight, understanding, wisdom and perspective.

It's the perfect state of existence and the most enriching state of being.

Every part of your life starts to become positive, productive and meaningful and, even when you experience static or disruption, the constant plug into the perspective of your soul allows you to see the shore beyond the storm much more clearly than before.

There is no more drama, no more paralysis, no more worry and anxiety and no more pain and regret, because you are looking into your soul, not your mind.

You are in control of this moment. It's your choice whether you want to try to steer the mind or swim in the soul.

CHAPTER 3

The Importance of Connectedness

YOUR SOUL IS PART OF EVERYTHING, and everything is part of your soul. All of the living world coexists and draws from the same energy source.

You are connected to this energy source through your soul, not your body.

Your mind and body are just the components that use this energy to allow you to function mentally and physically. Your mind and body do not create energy, nor do they replenish it. They simply draw from it, and your soul is the portal through which you have constant connection to this energy and the connectedness that is the living world.

If the soul is connected to everything and it is the portal through which we draw the energy to live – the life force that we refer to when describing our sense of vitality – then it makes sense that we are not and cannot be alone. We are eternally connected to all that is life and living, both human and the rest of the living world.

We are, through our souls, part of the connectedness that is the living world and the universe.

We may seem to have a unique corporeal form and our mind may tell us we are singular and separate, but that is only a physical expression of identity. We are physically unique, but our physical form is only a fraction of who we are.

But your mind naturally resists the idea of connectedness and shared universal energy. It has to in order to preserve its dominance. The purpose of your mind is to give you the information and functionality you need to be successful in your life.

But if you accept the idea of connectedness, suddenly your mind is minimized.

In other words, if there is a portal through which you can access another source of information unknown to your mind, then your mind becomes merely a life-support system, not a life-generator like it wants to be. It loses the control and governance it needs to conduct your life.

Your soul is not the least bit concerned about control – in fact, it facilitates the opposite in freedom and expression – but your mind exists to control.

Your mind needs to be in charge, to be the singular source of energy, information and vitality in your life, or it loses its bearings. Your mind wants to reject connectedness because connectedness violates its mission, to be the master of your existence.

The secret to creating a peaceful coexistence between your mind and your soul is to accept your soul connectedness without suppressing the functioning of your mind.

You can coexist with a soul that is the life-generator and a mind that is the life-support without changing one part of your mind's role in your life.

There is no drastic perceptual shift you need to make, no giant leap in self-awareness you have to take and no transforming belief system you have to accept to establish this coexistence.

It's just simple acknowledgement. Recognize that your mind is a life-support system but thinks that it is a life-generator. Let it do its job in giving you information and functioning to conduct your life and be grateful for its contributions.

There is no need to constrict your mind's work or judge its contributions because that just creates inner-tension.

The goal is not to supplant your mind with your soul. The goal is to accept coexistence and recognize that your soul has a much bigger and more active role in your life than you may have realized. The goal is to begin living in harmony with the contributions of your mind and the access to your soul.

It is and always has been your choice to listen to your thoughts or follow your intuition and now you know that what you may have referred to as a gut instinct or a hunch was actually your soul offering you a hint.

It was your soul being the portal that it is, offering you information that was not contained in your mind.

It was a supplement to the information you had in your mind's database that gave you more options and more perspective into a choice you needed to make.

Your gut instinct was not a fluke or an accident; it was an unconscious reaction to information you were seeking. Your hunch was not a baseless conclusion that you made. It was information that you absorbed outside the mental process.

Now imagine that you transform your gut instinct or hunch into a deliberate process.

If you accept the principle of connectedness to the energy and information that is the living world, then you can consciously tap into it whenever you want.

You don't have to wait for gut feelings and

hunches. You can find the information you need just by asking. That may seem trite and maybe even odd, but it is a natural conclusion to draw once you see your soul as the portal that it is.

Prayer and meditation do just that. They give you both direction and enlightenment through concentrated attention, and you typically ask a question, either articulated or implied, to receive it.

The only difference between consciously tapping into your soul connectedness and prayer and meditation is timing.

You reserve time to pray and meditate and you put yourself in a particular environment and mental state to do it. These are distinct activities that are structured and scheduled. Tapping into your soul connectedness for information is neither.

You don't have to make a point of asking your soul a question in order to receive information. And you don't have to be in a certain mental state or environment to ask and receive.

Recognizing that you have this portal is enough to tap into it. And recognizing that your soul exists outside of you, ungoverned by your mind, is enough awareness to receive the information you seek.

Everything you see, smell, hear and touch is a clue in your life. Every person you encounter, every conversation you hear or participate in, every circumstance you observe, these all contain information you have subconsciously asked for.

You may discount a lot of what you experience as inconsequential, but it is not.

Every experience can be mined for little nuggets of information that, when combined, illustrate the answer you were seeking.

Some of these clues are obvious, but most are not. The obvious clues are easy and are typically a projection of what you already expected or deduced in your mind. But the obvious clues are only a fraction of the whole picture or, better yet, whole answer to what you were seeking.

Put yourself in a recent situation during which you overheard something, or engaged in conversation with a stranger, and came away from the experience with information that was applicable to your life.

Maybe you were wondering where you could have a good meal with a certain dish or travel to on vacation or invest your money or look for a job. In any scenario, if you felt that you had received information that was applicable to your life, it's because you were seeking that information and it was probably congruent in timing and substance with what you were formulating in your mind.

In other words, there is nothing random about the information you receive. Whether you are subconsciously pondering a question or actively seeking information, you receive exactly what you seek.

The confusing part, though, is how you reconcile all the information that doesn't seem to apply to your life. It would be impossible to file away all the seemingly inconsequential information you encounter through your daily life for a later retrieval when the clue may have more relevance.

But that is the point. You don't have to file away anything.

The information was given to you through

your soul portal. It was not a transmission; it was a glimpse.

The information is permanently there, whether you internalized it or not. If you hear something today that seems irrelevant to your life, you will hear it again in some form when the relevance is more obvious.

We live our lives conditioned by time; the soul does not. The energy and information that is the living world is not governed by time.

The past, present and future all simultaneously exist without any regard for calendars, clocks and schedules.

We seem to live a linear life, but, actually, we do not.

We live in a circle. All that we are doing and will do in the future is occurring simultaneously. I know this is a radical concept, but so is déjà vu and the sense of uncanny familiarity when you meet someone and feel you already know him/her.

You are living your life and accumulating experiences in a circular way, not through a linear projection.

What seems like uncanny familiarity to you is just a mind perception. It is not uncanny. It is a connection you asked for either subconsciously or consciously at some point and you were given it.

Now you see it in the physical world for what seems like the first time, so it feels new, but familiar. It is not new and it has been familiar since you asked for it.

So, back to the inconsequential information you encounter that doesn't seem relevant in your life. If you can accept the non-time that is the living world, then you can accept that everything you experience and encounter has relevance. It's simply a matter of when.

It is not necessary to take inventory of all you see, hear, smell and touch. All you need is recognition.

Recognize that there is no randomness in the living world and that you are given information that you ask for, and, if you just observe the experience and all the information associated with it, you will have absorbed it.

It's a subtle soul snapshot you are taking. It's

not a mental process in which you observe something and try to align the experience with what you know and can analyze. It's just recognition.

It's just resolving to be present every moment of your life and taking note of all that you experience.

Of course, your mind will not be happy about this because it wants you to identify with its thoughts and feelings, not what it considers the random present moment variables that are your experiences.

Your mind needs you to pay attention to its thoughts so it can "properly" govern your life. It needs your full attention.

But, as we learned earlier, it will be just fine without your attention, so let it do what it does well in thought, while you do what is more enriching in soul – being present.

The other paradigm of connectedness is what we label as extrasensory perception, the ability to predict the future and see an experience that we are not involved in.

Society has come to label this ability as paranormal or, simply put, outside the realm of normal. It does seem that the ability of extrasensory perception is outside our normal senses, but this is really a function of semantics.

We use our senses as tools to help our mind and body function in the physical world, so any ability to perceive or interpret things outside the physical world is naturally going to be considered "not normal."

But extrasensory perception is actually as normal as seeing, hearing, touching and smelling.

The ability to see experiences remotely from ourselves and in another time is simply a function of our connectedness.

If we are accessing the soul portal for information and mining its clues to answer our questions, then it is natural that we will see anything in the living world that we want to see.

Remember, the living world is not governed by time; there is no linear movement of energy, just the circular existence of all the experiences associated with our lives.

Time as past, present and future does not exist in the soul domain, so time does not govern what we can see when we are tapped into it. Time does, however, govern our mind and its thoughts, so anything we perceive not of this time will naturally be counterintuitive to our mental process.

But that's okay. And that's the point.

The goal is to be counterintuitive where our mind is concerned, because real intuition resides in the soul.

We are not violating any natural laws by tapping into the soul portal. Indeed, we are abiding by them when we seek information beyond our mind's information store.

Thus, if you see an experience that foretells the future or perceive a circumstance happening outside of your life, you've confirmed that you are tapped into the soul portal.

We all have this ability and we can all nurture this ability. We just have to take the first step, which is what we covered in the last two chapters – accepting the duality of the mind and soul and being conscious of what we're doing right now.

Only the inhibition of your mind and its relationship with time and physical world senses can impose limits on how much insight, understanding, wisdom and perspective you can receive.

It's not about predicting the future and seeing circumstances remote from you. It's about tapping into unlimited information and enriching your life with it.

If you pick up some clues about the future in the process, it's just a by-product of your immersion in the soul portal. It's not extraordinary or paranormal. It's simply connectedness.

Finally, the other correlation to the energy and information that is the living world is our ability to perform extraordinary physical feats during a crisis.

We have all heard stories of people doing unbelievable things to save a loved one's life, like picking up a car on one end or physically defending a family member threatened with violence in an extremely unmatched situation, but there is no scientific explanation for where this energy and strength comes from other than correlations to adrenaline production and "fight or flight" stimuli.

But these correlations don't explain how we can manipulate our body to do things that it could not do in normal situations. The real explanation is being present and connected to the unlimited energy source.

In a crisis situation, even your mind is focused just on the present circumstances to resolve the conflict without any harm to yourself or someone you care for. It is not distracting you at that moment with its endless thought generation and life governance. It is completely focused on surviving and protecting.

Thus, you can be fully aware and present without any distractions or competing thoughts. This hyper-awareness automatically plugs you into the soul portal and, thus, a direct feed into the unlimited energy source.

This energy is converted into strength for your body and, now, all three – your mind, body and soul – are aligned and focused on resolving the threatening situation. Sure, there is excess adrenaline production that facilitates the strength, but adrenaline alone is not capable of producing strength that exceeds your anatomical limits. It is the unlimited energy that is the living world that you are tapped into that allows you to exceed your body's capabilities.

In that moment, you become more than your physical presence. You become the energy. And when the situation is resolved, you return to "normal."

The portal remains open but you go back to the dual existence of mind and soul and the co-existence of thought and insight. The energy returns to the source and the living world remains fully enriched.

That is how we participate in the unlimited energy and information that is the living world.

That is connectedness.

CHAPTER 4

Personal Power

THE GOAL OF SPIRITUAL DEVELOPMENT is personal empowerment. When you understand the mechanics of the mind and the potential of the soul, you are liberated from the automatic currents that govern your life.

You become the captain of your own ship and you can regulate what thoughts you will identify with and how they will affect you. You are empowered when you can experience a feeling or an emotion and not identify with it.

You may feel physically sick or emotionally

distraught, but, through empowerment, you can isolate these sensations as natural components of your mind/body relationship. They are not your identity and they are not related to who you are or who you will become.

To understand that our mind and body are mere vessels which we use to navigate the physical world and that our soul is the true wellspring of all our potential is true liberation. And this liberation is the foundation of empowerment.

Now you need to build on this foundation of empowerment through the understanding of three things: The difference between want and desire, the power of detachment and the elimination of good and bad.

All three perspectives give you the tools you need to decipher what emanates from your soul and what is generated from your mind.

When you can recognize with precision and clarity what is enriching and what is acquisitive, you will have the ability to choose, and choice is the essence of empowerment.

Likewise, when you can remove yourself from

the drama and triteness that our world can be and still feel connected, you will become the steward of your life's experiences.

And when you can accept all your situations and circumstances without qualification or judgment, you will have reached the summit of perspective and insight.

WANT AND DESIRE

Desire is the language of the soul, while want is the parlance of the mind.

Our mind needs to acquire, dominate, control and manipulate, and it requires things, relationships and experiences to accomplish this.

Our mind wants to acquire possessions, people and experiences so it can feel in control and rich: The more possessions, people and experiences, the better chance of achieving success.

We want that car because it connotes luxury or recreation. We want that girl/guy in our life because we want her/his looks or possessions or her/his attention to fill voids. We want that trip abroad because we want recreation or travel experience or the opportunity to see more of the world.

There is nothing wrong with any of these wants, just the intention that drives them.

We want because we are seeking completion, and we are acquisitive because the more possessions, people and experiences we have in our lives, the more we feel in control of our destiny and our ability to achieve success.

We don't feel complete without the things we want because, according to our minds, they are the resources we need to achieve and be successful. And, when we get the things we want, we become possessive and jealous of them. We can't afford to lose them and we will defend them from potential repossession or loss.

Our lives become an inventory of our possessions, people and experiences, and we come to define ourselves by them.

The object, relationship or situation becomes more than just something we possess; it becomes our identity. Instead of enjoying the pleasure we can derive from the things we want, we allow them to take over and become powerful influences on how we live and think about our lives.

We lose perspective on the transitory nature of possessions, the short-term pleasure they generate, and, when they deteriorate or fade away, we replace them without any assessment of the true impact they had in our lives.

Our wants become driven by a fear of loss instead of a need for pleasure. Our mind-based acquisitiveness becomes the control and our lives become the governed.

Desire, on the other hand, emanates from the soul. It is a genuine longing to bring something into your life that will enrich you in important, lasting ways. Desire is a deeply felt pull toward things that will complement your vision for your life. It is not acquisitive like want.

Yes, desire can be for possessions, relationships and experiences, but the intention is the opposite of want.

Desire is about creating symmetry and opportunity in your life so you can fully develop your potential. It is about enhancing your understanding and perspective by drawing resources into your life that will facilitate your growth and development.

Want is about acquisition and utility, whereas desire is about receiving and growth.

One example of desire is a change in geography to a place that feels more comfortable and inspiring.

You desire to move to reconstitute your life with new opportunity and scenery that will help you redirect your energy into those areas that may have been neglected. A change in place allows you to reform your identity and perspective and recast your potential in a new and exciting way.

Your desire for a change in place is a lasting commitment to resettle and redefine your life in important ways. It is not something you want, but something you long to become.

Your desire for a change in place is your desire for personal growth.

Another example of desire is education. When you desire to learn, you desire growth and the opportunity to gain insight, understanding, wisdom and perspective. Your desire to learn is a commitment to better understand your world and your prospects within it. It is a commitment to personal development and empowerment.

When you desire to learn, you are engaging your soul and your potential. It is impossible to want to learn because want is a short-term acquisitive process that does not require commitment.

Only desire will give you the discipline and perseverance you need to commit yourself to learning and the growth it will generate in you.

Finally, relationships are based on desire. To desire someone in your life is to feel the need to give, to love through empathy and attention, to create a space where you can share your life with another person.

When you desire a relationship, it's because you desire happiness, not a transient, want-based pleasure that will eventually fade, leaving little tangible value in your life.

You can't *want* a relationship, because a relationship is about long-term commitment, not short-term acquisition. If you want anything related to a relationship, it is typically companionship in which you combine similar traits, abilities and perspectives into a unit that enjoys time and experiences together.

There is nothing wrong with this want if it is seen for what it is. To desire a relationship, however, is to desire long-term companionship and the opportunity to grow and develop in concert with another person.

There is no short-term value in this commitment, only long-term desire and dedication.

A relationship is about the symmetry of giving and receiving and the sincerity of sharing. It is about creating something beyond yourself and sustaining a bond through energy and attention – energy and attention you can only channel through desire.

Desire is empowering because it is a direct connection to the unlimited potential of the soul.

Desire is the portal through which we draw from the endless energy and information that is the living world because desire is the language of the soul.

We can only grow and develop through desire, and we can only gain the insight, understanding, wisdom and perspective we need to be truly happy through desire.

Your combined desires in your life are your commitment to yourself to live a life of potential.

And this potential is empowerment.

POWER OF DETACHMENT

Life is rooted in both connectedness and detachment, living as part of the energy and information that is the living world, but apart from the circumstances and realities of the physical world.

We can feel fully connected to all that is our world, but we don't have to subscribe to the titles and mantels that are applied to the canvas of our life.

Connectedness is the door through which all the opportunities of our life will pass and detachment is the liberation from the mark they will leave.

We can be fully engaged in the world and mine all the opportunity and success that we can, but we don't have to identify with the recognition and accolades that we collect in the process. We can be proud of what we achieve but still not define ourselves by these achievements.

This power to separate ourselves from what we receive yet still appreciate it is the bedrock of perspective. When you can truly see yourself as detached and growing with unlimited opportunity, you no longer need the distinctions and labels that accrue to you through your actions in the world.

You can build the world's largest building, but your building is the achievement, not your success. Your success is the endeavor itself, the creativity and commitment you had which will benefit others.

You can be elected into public office, but your election is not the success; it is the vehicle through which you have the opportunity to do productive, creative and positive things for others.

You may be called by a certain title, but the title is irrelevant when compared to the success you can achieve through your ability to positively impact other lives.

You can start a family and raise wonderful children with all kinds of abilities and potential, but your children are not your success.

Your commitment to imbuing your children with the morality, judgment and ambition to become good people is your success.

The good things your children may achieve in their lives do reflect well on you, but you derive your satisfaction from knowing you imparted to your children the energy and information they needed to develop into positive people.

Detachment is the art of engaging in the world, but not deriving identity from the experience.

Detachment is about a long-term commitment to personal development and growth without any need for the labels and mantels of success.

It's an appreciation of what you do and how

you impact the world without a need for the recognition.

When you are detached, you are spiritually-identified and free to pursue your desires without the static of the mind-based need for credit and reward.

Detachment is empowerment because your success comes from within, not reflected from without.

Detachment from what we perceive as failure is equally as important.

Our lives are full of goals and ambitions and we tend to measure ourselves by how many of them we achieve. We label the fruition of these goals and ambitions as success. But, as we concluded earlier, success is not the matriculation of our actions, but the action itself and the passion we invest in it.

Thus, if success comes from within, then the non-achievement of a goal or ambition must also come from the same source and be just as important in our lives.

True detachment is not associating ourselves with either the success or the failure of our goals and ambitions.

We can only acknowledge the truth that becomes our lives when we take stock of what has become a reality and what has not.

In other words, our spiritual development hinges on the perspective that whatever happens in our lives is a product of our true desires, and that if something does not happen that we'd hoped would, we have to revisit our wants and desires and assess their authenticity to see what is the true reality that we desire in our lives.

This sounds like a complicated and confusing process, but, as you'll see in the next chapter, it's actually a very simple "past inventory" that will prove the perfection of our desires and our ability to manifest those true desires in our lives.

Detachment from both what we label as success and failure is the spiritual currency of empowerment. We are not defined by success or failure and we are not identified by the results of either.

We are empowered by understanding that

our life is taking shape as we truly desire and that what may seem like a failure is simply a course correction or change in path.

Our mind will color the experience of a failure with anxiety and fear because the mind is success oriented, but our soul will embrace the failure as an evolution into the next experience that we truly desire.

Because the mind is louder and more effective at getting our attention, the failure will resonate with anxiety and fear and we will blame ourselves for those goals and ambitions that do not become reality.

But, if we tap into our soul portal and assess the failure for what it is, it is clear that we are evolving toward the path we truly desire.

We have the choice to peer into our soul for guidance and ignore the suggestion of our mind that we must panic and feel regret. This choice is detachment and this detachment is empowerment.

Finally, detachment is freedom from external affirmation. External affirmation is the process of seeking approval from familiar and unfamiliar people in our lives to justify our thoughts and actions. We are imbued with this impulse for seeking approval at an early age as personal development in our youth is a function of parental, adult, teacher and peer approval.

The more approval we win, the stronger our self-esteem and the better our prospects for success. We carry this perspective into adulthood because personal development as an adult is a function of partner, colleague, supervisor and peer approval.

We find the right mate, earn the trust of our coworkers, gain career advancement and enjoy social opportunities according to how much we please others.

Our thoughts and actions have to align on some level with what is acceptable to the people in our lives if we are to have any momentum toward our goals and ambitions. We cannot achieve success unless we have the support and approval of those in our lives who have some impact or influence over us.

This is the accepted view of external affirmation, but it is not valid.

Our goal in interpersonal relationships should not be to please others, but to make others feel comfortable in our presence.

We are not obligated to think only those thoughts and do only those actions that meet the approval of the people in our lives, but we are obligated to think those thoughts and do those actions that do not trespass against others.

As long as we do not threaten others with our thoughts and actions, we are free to invest our lives in our own desires and passions. We may be considered different from accepted social norms, but, as long as we are focused on positive evolutions in our lives, we won't be considered a threat.

In fact, if we develop our lives with true desire and sensitivity, we will actually inspire others to consider their own personal development and growth and maybe even alternate paths that could bring them more opportunities for success and fulfillment.

Thus, living a life that is not dependent on the approval and endorsement of others is not rebellion or even non-conformity. It is simply a parallel path on which you are fueled by your own sense of enrichment and opportunity.

When you are not defined by the impressions of others, you are not restricted by their expectations for your life. You are liberated from the traditional path and free to find your individual path that is based on your personal desires and passions.

And you can walk your own path and still mine the riches and opportunities of the world around you. You don't need to conform to succeed; you just need the self-awareness to invest yourself in actions that will bring you what you desire while not trespassing on the paths of others.

When you have the self-awareness to live a unique and authentic life, free from the need for external affirmation, you are liberated and unlimited in your potential.

You are detached from the yoke of acceptance and endowed with the perspective you need to develop and grow along the path of your choosing.

This detachment is ultimate empowerment because, not only are you cultivating your own desires and passions, you are inspiring others to consider the same.

Living an authentic life based on desire is much more compelling to people in your life than unconscious conformity. If you're detached, yet sensitive and focused, you have become a true center of power for yourself and others.

The potential you have created for yourself and have inspired in others is unlimited. You have combined empowerment with connectedness and that is the ultimate state of being.

GOOD AND BAD

Similar to detachment, the elimination of good and bad is an important component of your personal power.

Good and bad are labels like success and failure that distract you from your true identity, and when you identify more with the label than the underlying meaning in a circumstance or experience, you undermine the effectiveness of your true desire.

In other words, when you reach a moment that you label good or bad, you are focused more on your reaction to the moment than its importance and, thus, distract yourself from the true meaning of that moment in your life.

This type of assessment is counterproductive to the process and intent of investing your desires.

Unfortunately, social convention is based on the labels of good and bad, and we are conditioned to label each circumstance and situation as such to properly categorize it in our minds.

If something is bad, avoid it in the future. If something is good, remember it so you can replicate it in the future or retrieve the positive memory for another positive feeling. Both labels, as you can see, involve the mind and the future.

When you label something good or bad, you

are unconsciously preparing yourself for the future so you can either replicate the experience or avoid it in similar circumstances.

But the future does not exist, and the mind, and especially the memory, is unreliable. If we live our lives by labels, we are conditioning ourselves to focus on the future rather than the present moment.

This wastes energy and distracts us from the meaning of the present moment and, ultimately, our path and desires.

There is no value in applying and remembering labels because labels are only a conduit into the future. They have no value or applicability to the present moment, and they do nothing to affirm your identity or the effectiveness of your desires.

This is especially applicable to the label bad. Labeling something good glosses over the opportunity to assess the meaning of the moment and how your desires are manifesting in your life, but labeling something bad completely derails any perspective you could have on the present.

We naturally want to avoid things that are labeled bad, especially if they are causing pain or loss, because we are conditioned for self-preservation and survival. Our mind will quickly extricate us from a painful situation with the application of the label bad and a strong reaction to the circumstance.

This may be an important reaction, and integral to your immediate survival if the circumstance could cause harm to your body, but it is a distracting reaction if the moment is not threatening your survival and you have the opportunity to assess the moment and what it may mean in your life.

In either case, however, whether the situation requires immediate extrication or not, there is no need to apply the label bad either at that moment or when it passes.

Even if it is clear the moment was threatening your life, there is unlimited opportunity for growth and perspective in the post-analysis of that moment that can only happen if it is not filed away as bad.

Once it's filed away as bad, you will avoid

revisiting it, thus losing the opportunity for self development and growth.

Labeling a moment as bad relegates it to a bad memory that should be avoided. Not labeling it as bad gives you the opportunity to assess it for the meaning it has in your life.

Let's look at an example we've probably all encountered. You are sitting on the airplane alone in your aisle content to have your free space for the flight. Minutes before the front door closes and the airplane is released, another passenger boards and sits right beside you. You are annoyed that you just lost your space, but still calm enough to enjoy the flight.

As soon as the passenger sits down, he turns to you and attempts to strike up a conversation. You offer quick replies as you are more interested in rest than talking, but your neighbor continues.

This goes on – the conversational attempts and your short, disinterested replies – for quite some time. Nothing the passenger says is resonating with you and you are becoming increasingly annoyed that your physical and mental space have been violated.

This situation is bad because you have three hours to endure with this distraction.

But then you change your attitude and your perspective and decide that there is meaning in every moment in your life and that people, things and experiences come into your life to facilitate your desires.

You start concentrating on what your neighbor is offering in his conversational attempts and it takes just seconds for you to realize that you have a lot in common.

In fact, within minutes, you realize you have met someone who is not only a good connection in your profession, but a very likeable person you can relate to. You spend the remainder of the flight engaged in conversation with this person and, when you land, exchange contact information to keep in touch.

You get off the flight having transformed a situation you initially labeled as bad into something that has left a positive and affirming impact on your life.

You recognize now that labels are distractions from the opportunity of the moment and you resolve to begin assessing your moments for their meaning rather than dismissing them if they conflict with your expectation of the situation.

This resolve to not label your moment is empowering and this empowerment can only facilitate your true desires in the next.

Personal power is the ability to distinguish between want and desire, detach yourself from the identity of success and failure and avoid the labels of good and bad.

All three abilities remove you from the physical, temporal realm and put you in an elevated place of perspective.

When you can see the difference between passion and pleasure, growth and credit and meaning and labels, you have achieved self-awareness and insight that will transform your participation in the moments of your life from passive experience to engineered purpose.

In the next chapter, we will explore how a simple shift in perspective will allow you to apply meaning to these distinctions and give you the tools to begin using them in your life.

Even if these previous chapters make sense and you accept the meaning of these concepts, you still deserve proof that you have, and *always have* had, the ability to engineer all the moments of your life.

I will give you this proof and, when you are done reading, you will see that you are self-aware and insightful enough to do this consciously for the rest of your life.

The secret is you already are living your life in that elevated place of perspective and you have the insight, understanding and wisdom to live fully engaged, enriched and aware.

You're just one blink away from knowing it.

CHAPTER 5

Practical Mysticism

PRACTICAL MYSTICISM is the exercise of incorporating this elevated perspective of self-awareness into your life and, through detachment, desire and non-judgment, engineering your life exactly how you like.

There is no perennial secret to the art of mysticism, just the faith that you have the ability and insight to cultivate all you desire from the energy and information that is the living world.

We tend to think of mysticism as an occult or magical practice that requires special spiritual capacity and other-world senses, but that is not the case.

Through the years, as we organized spiritual practices into congregational religions and belief systems, we consciously and unconsciously marginalized mysticism as something unrelated to the belief in a Creator and Creation.

We distilled the art of divine manifestation from our faith practices and, thus, lost faith in our ability to partner with Creation (our world) to create in our own lives those circumstances and experiences that manifest our true desires.

The result is that religion and mysticism now exist in separate – though parallel – realms, with very little cross-over in our modern world.

We have created divisions in ourselves based on how we perceive the living world and its source and, thus, have tampered with the spiritual connectedness that we are, and should be, to manifest the lives we desire.

These divisions have become so accepted and mainstream in our modern world that we view any suggestion of unification – the reunification of mysticism and religion – as counter-religious.

But it is exactly the opposite.

Your belief in God or a Higher Power, regardless of how you perceive of and approach this belief, is proof that you already have the spiritual capacity and, thus, the proper perspective on mysticism to become a partner in Creation and not just its subject.

Now, here's the proof.

PAST INVENTORY

Concentrate on the detachment, desire and non-judgment of living positively and in the moment that we described earlier. Quiet your mind and its ego and look into your past.

Focus on a circumstance or experience that you considered bad or painful and make an inventory of how you arrived at that moment and how you emerged from it.

Be very honest and humble in your assessments of this past event.

Extract all the emotions and feelings that you

might have experienced at that time and look at the impact it had on your life, then and now.

Don't leave any detail untouched in your inventory process; fully re-live it and take mental notes of all the features and implications that it contained.

Now, ask yourself this one question: Did I desire that to happen? Your first reaction will be a firm "No" because why would you desire anything to come into your life that would cause pain and disruption?

Certainly you would not consciously engineer a moment in your life that would be hurtful...but maybe you would unconsciously. In other words, what you *desired* to happen did happen, and what you *wanted* to happen did not.

Let's look at an example. A friend shared with me recently that he had left his previous town more miserable than he had ever been in his life.

He explained that this was due to a break-up with his girlfriend. And not just a normal break-up; she had suddenly left their home without any discussion or clue that it was coming. There was no communication for months following her departure, and, shortly before he left town, my friend found out that she was seriously involved with another man.

Now, that is truly painful.

It would seem there could be no want/desire inventory to take here. This was just a bad event in his life that he did not have any control over. Or did he?

My first question to him was to describe what had attracted him to her in the first place. He offered the normal points of symmetry that we all look for in a romantic partner and, on the surface, it seemed to be a good fit.

I then asked what he was not attracted to in her. He did not hesitate a moment before responding that she was just plain mean.

He gave me some pretty startling examples of how indifferent and cruel she could be and, in the process, he relived the emotional pain he had felt in those situations where he was the victim of her cruelty.

I asked if her cruelty had been enough for him to consider breaking up with her, and he said "of course."

There is the intersection of want and desire.

He truly wanted her in his life for romantic partnership and he was genuinely attracted to her in many ways, but he did not want the cruelty that came with the relationship.

He "secretly" desired to find another woman who was kind, but he did not take any conscious steps to end the relationship and find this kinder woman.

He engaged in the relationship with this woman based on his wants and endured her cruelty despite his desires, and, therefore, the relationship ended without his participation.

He received exactly what he desired – to be out of a relationship that involved cruelty – and he was now free to find another woman that was kind.

At the time, however, he did not view life through the prism of want vs. desire and spiritual connectedness. He did not understand that we create the experiences we desire.

He saw life as a series of events, circumstances and experiences that randomly happened, sometimes with our contributions, but mostly due to variables beyond our control.

But when I offered this past inventory – want/desire perspective to him, he immediately saw it.

He may have felt pain due to the break-up, but now he can see the pain as strictly illusory and mind-based because he had achieved what he truly desired, to be free to find another relationship based on compassion, not cruelty.

Had he been living consciously during that time in his life, he could have been proactive in this relationship resolution and saved himself the pain of the sudden separation.

This past inventory proved to my friend that he was in control of his life, and he went on to assess other past events that had caused him pain. His success rate in extricating desire from the web of want and, thus, proving his ability to control his own life was perfect.

Today he views life as something he can engineer, and he is steadily learning the art of consciously making his next moment a reflection of his true desire.

I'll now offer you a very personal example of a past event in my life that I used as my litmus test to prove to myself that I have the ability to manifest my life exactly how I desire. I selected this particular event because it was the most painful and deconstructing time that I had ever endured.

It took me years to regain perspective after this event and an enormous amount of energy to reconstruct my life along a new path. If there was ever a death in life, this was it for me.

Even when I reconciled the loss I felt years later, I still could not understand how this could have happened to me.

Everything I had ever known or thought I would become was disrupted and lost. To me, it seemed like a black hole I would live with for the rest of my life.

But, today, living consciously, the event has become my wishing well.

This is where I travel back to now when I

need to remind myself that I can manifest the life I desire, and that what seems bad now is really a change in path that will take me to where I truly need to be.

It's because of this event that I have my true identity. What I lost was an illusion. What I gained was real and everlasting.

And now this event has become something to share as proof that we are in full control of our lives.

I was born into an aviation family of several generations. One of my first childhood memories is of my father pulling me up into the cockpit of his fighter aircraft and letting me sit in the seat, marveling at all the gauges and instruments. I was four, but I still remember the experience vividly. I remember making a commitment to myself right then that I would become a fighter pilot, and I would dedicate my life to doing whatever I had to do to achieve this goal.

For the next 15 years, I focused intently on my academic performance, striving to earn an ROTC scholarship and, ultimately, the opportunity to compete for acceptance into Air Force flight training.

I won the scholarship and then dedicated myself through college to winning the slot into pilot training. I won that too, and not just regular pilot training, but the world's most advanced and competitive flight training program which accepted only a few American pilot candidates each year to train with our international allies.

I entered the flight training program confident that I had reached the summit from which I would certainly achieve my lifelong goal.

I dedicated myself to my aviation studies and flight assignments over the next two years and, as I approached the end of the program, I was overwhelmed with a sense of accomplishment that I had honored my lifelong commitment to becoming a fighter pilot.

But just weeks before graduation, the Air Force eliminated all the assignments into fighter aircraft due to ongoing budget cuts.

My class, along with many others that were trained to transition into fighters, were assigned to other aircraft types or given staff jobs to reduce the training expense of follow-on fighter training. I was fortunate to be assigned to another aircraft type and not given a staff job that would take me out of the aviation world.

With the goal of reapplying for a fighter training slot, I immediately committed myself to becoming the best pilot possible in this non-fighter aircraft and volunteered for as much additional duty as I could over the next two years to make myself as competitive as possible for my reapplication into fighters.

I chose to view this non-fighter assignment as a hurdle, not the end of my dream. I just knew that all my years of genuine focus and sincere effort towards achieving this goal would get me to the finish line.

It didn't happen. I exhausted every possible avenue that might get me back into a fighter aircraft, but, in the end, I had to accept that, due to the budget cuts, I was not going to realize my dream.

I accepted an early separation from the Air Force, which was part of the budget cuts at the time, and went on with my life outside of military aviation. I started a very meaningful career a few months later and invested myself in the opportunities I would find on this path towards reconstructing my identity. I was determined to evolve gracefully and move on.

I tried, but I was not successful.

In my mind, I could not accept this failure. It seemed impossible to me that I could have had this singular purpose in my life for so many years without fulfilling it.

I didn't know the distinction between want and desire at the time, but I instinctively knew that a lifetime of passion and focus had to be the ingredients of true desire and enough to realize a dream, especially when I had achieved everything I was supposed to towards this goal.

I was confused and lost and my self-identity was depleted. I didn't feel I would ever recover from this change of path in my life. I spent many years in this state of self-identity limbo, with no answers as to why and how this could have happened.

And then I began my spiritual transformation, my growth into conscious, self-aware living. I committed myself to living a life free of regret and anxiety, and I invested all my energy into absorbing information that offered clues on how to achieve this.

I connected myself into the energy and information of the living world and found spiritual resources and opportunities that I had never known existed.

I was truly energized to begin seeing my life take shape based on my desires, and I was thrilled by the prospects of what I could achieve and become with this new perspective and insight.

But the nagging thought of my military aviation goal and how it did not manifest in my life would not go away.

If I had found this truth that we are in control of our lives, then it seemed impossible that I had not achieved this lifelong desire.

There was no way that a commitment I made to myself at an early age, combined with a lifetime of academic and military achievement towards that commitment, could have failed to manifest into the realization of my dream.

If there was ever desire, this was it – a lifetime of singular purpose and focus towards achieving one goal.

So I developed this system of past inventory to try to isolate the variables that had contributed to my not being assigned to a fighter aircraft.

I looked at the experience of my flight training from every angle and made honest mental notes about what I liked and did not like, but I still came up short.

I could not find any clues as to how such deeply invested passion and desire had not manifested in my life.

So I called my brother, who I'd called frequently during my flight training time, to see if I might have relayed something to him that would be a clue as to why my desire did not manifest.

The conversation lasted about a minute. "You loved the flying, but hated the mission," he told me. He reminded me that all our conversations during that time were based on my distaste for the aggressive nature of fighter-type flying vs. my love for the precision and skill of military aviation.

He cited numerous examples of missions I'd shared with him during which the speed and flight parameters had made me more nervous than energized and more disconnected from the flying environment than excited to be in the air.

The bottom line was that I loved serving as a pilot, but I did not enjoy the adrenaline of flying fighters.

And then I saw through the mist: My desire was to attend flight training and serve my country; my ego was sitting in that fighter aircraft.

My lifelong desire was to fly like my father and grandfather had, in uniform and for our country; the desire was not for speed or danger. It never had been. And it never has been since.

My mind, or, more specifically, my ego had converted my desire into its own conduit for recognition and I'd never seen the link.

But now I do.

I achieved my desire, every part of it. I graduated from military flight training; I served my country in uniform; I continued a family aviation tradition; and I proved to myself that I could accomplish a very difficult goal.

The process was perfect. I had manifested exactly what I had desired.

What seemed like a failure to me for all those years is now proof that I have always been in control of my life. I have always been capable of seeding my destiny with my desires and cultivating all the experiences and resources I needed in my life to bring me happiness and opportunity.

What broke apart my self-identity at that time turns out to be the most important turning point in my life, now and then.

I am on the right path, and I have created the identity I have always desired, neither of which could have happened had I achieved what I wanted instead of what I desired.

Now I want to offer you a more recent personal example of the power of past inventory as proof that we have the ability to control our lives and our circumstances.

As I introduced in the beginning of the book, I have stretched myself and all my resources over the past four years to make this entrepreneurial venture of building aviation terminals a reality.

It has taken four times as long as I had anticipated, which has naturally depleted me financially. I am in financial peril and teetering on worst case scenario if the venture does not matriculate in the very near future.

Of course, my desire when I began this venture was to make it to project funding financially whole, so what is the meaning of this financial peril?

Surely I desired to both create something in the aviation world and remain financially viable. Only a fool would desire to be successful in achieving a professional goal but only at the cost of insolvency.

My desire was perfectly bifurcated between professional and financial success, so why am I in this uncomfortable situation now?

The answer is because I have other desires that are evolving and this situation is just a way station in that process.

My process of inventory taught me that.

EVOLUTIONARY AND ACHIEVEMENT DESIRE

We have two types of desire, one based on evolution and the other based on achievement.

Evolutionary desires are related to personal growth and self development – refining personality traits and perspectives to make us more effective and aware in our lives.

Achievement desires deal with manifesting something tangible in our lives like a rewarding profession, a lasting relationship, a new house, a trip abroad, etc.

Both desires have value – there is no hierarchy which determines how our desires will manifest in our lives.

You can have parallel evolutionary and achievement desires that may affect each other, but, in the end, both can be cultivated into reality without one diminishing the other.

That is the case with my financial peril.

My achievement desire four years ago was to build aviation terminals. That desire has not changed and my success is still being manifested.

I also had an evolutionary desire at that time that I focused on very strongly as it would be a major course correction for me and my life.

I wanted to learn patience and respect for money, two perspectives I had not done well with through my life.

Both my achievement and evolutionary desires were planted at the same time, and I am now approaching the realization of both.

I'm on the cusp of concluding the investment process for my venture and my relationship with money and time has drastically changed over the past four years.

I see money now as a facilitator, not the host – a means to buy time to do the things I want in this life.

And I see time as a conduit, not a hurdle – a vessel in which things germinate and develop on their own schedule but always to the benefit of the one waiting for them.

I have learned respect for money and patience because I desired it and they manifested into my current circumstances.

I could not have learned the meaning of money and the impact of time unless both were very salient features in my life and, in a prolonged period of self-investment where financial resources and dynamic project schedules mean everything, I've had the perfect opportunity.

My evolutionary desires of respect for money and patience and my achievement desire to build aviation terminals were separate at birth, conjoined as they manifested, and will be unique realities at their conclusion.

It was a simple inventory process to see this and a rewarding exercise to distill the anxiety out of financial peril and replace it with confirmation that I've manifested an evolutionary desire that has had no impact on the achievement desire it happened to share space with.

Of course, my next desire is financial stability. I've earned enough stripes where respect for money and patience are concerned.

MANIFESTING OUR DESIRES

Hopefully your past inventory was successful in proving that you have always been in control of your life, even if it's been unconsciously.

I hope you found the distinction between want and desire to be real and can see now that all you've ever desired has manifested in your life in some form.

This is a very important first step in spiritual perspective, and it's your proof that you are connected to the living world in ways you might not have realized until now.

It is your starting point in practical mysticism – the recognition that you are participating in your personal development and growth and that you have the spiritual capacity to continue this development through experiences, circumstances and resources that you will bring into your life to make your desires come true.

Now it's time to take the past inventory forward, to seed your present moment with the same perspective that was revealed in your past desire assessments and make your present reality and your next moment exactly how you like.

Manifesting our desires starts with self-awareness. We have to see the distinction between the physical world around us and the unseen world that we live in through our soul.

As we discussed earlier, our mind and body occupy the physical world while our soul is eternally free and connected to all the energy and information that is the living world, what we can perceive with our senses and what we can't.

Thus, our soul is the conduit through which we seed our desires to manifest in our lives. If we are present in a soul-like way and aware that we are in this state of being, we can deposit our desires in the energy and information of the living world and allow the natural process of manifestation to begin.

This may seem a little arcane, to be present in a soul-like way and deposit your desires in the energy and information of the living world, but you actually do it everyday.

Every time you pray, meditate or focus, you

are depositing a desire into a space you can't see, hoping for positive results to come into your life.

What I am suggesting is to be conscious of the action, the source of the deposit and the results you anticipate.

To be present in a soul-like way is the same thing as prayer, meditation and focus – it just requires more attention to the process of depositing a desire.

This attention to the process requires your participation, and awareness of your participation is critical to replicating the process again when you deposit another desire.

The awareness of your participation is what gives you the confidence in your spiritual ability to manifest your desires in your life, and this confidence is the foundation for happiness.

In other words, if you truly believe you have the capacity to shape your life as you desire then there is no limit to what you can bring into your life to make you happy.

Now, let's define in a little more detail what it means to be present in a soul-like way.

When we are present in a physical way, we are conscious of our senses, what we can see, hear, touch, smell and feel, and we have heightened awareness of all the stimuli that are interacting with our senses in the environment around us.

This is sometimes referred to as hyper-sensitivity, where every nuance of the environment is perceived in vivid definition and context.

This type of physical awareness requires an enormous amount of energy as every part of our body and our mind is working on analyzing an infinite number of stimuli and variables towards calculating the appropriate physical response to our environment.

On the other side, to be present in a soul-like way is to be released from all physical awareness and the stimuli of our environment.

In a soul-like state of being, we are focused only on the empty space around us, the calm that exists outside of the physical world and our temporal environment.

In this state of being, we are focused only on what we cannot perceive and that which we cannot assess. There is nothing for our mind and body to do in this soul-like state and this inability to participate naturally relaxes them, allowing us to connect with our soul without interruption.

And once we achieve this connection with our soul, there is nothing for us to do but be aware that we are connected.

All the energy and information that we need to manifest our desires is being transferred automatically; there is nothing required of us to receive it but our consciousness that we are connected to it.

That is a soul-like state of being and that is where the potential of our life resides.

Now that we are aware of the source from which we manifest our lives, the energy and information that we find in a soul-like state of being, we need to understand the power of being positive.

We live in a very jaded world where conflict, drama and pain have become the bedrock of our relationships, interactions and entertainment.

Emotions like anger, frustration, anxiety, jealousy, hatred and indifference have become natural components of our lives, and we accept them as normal and sometimes even necessary to function in the world.

Unless we live on a mountaintop or on a remote island, it seems impossible to exist and function in the world without subscribing to the negativity that has come to define it.

But we have a choice and that choice is perspective.

We can choose to view the world through our minds and make mind-based decisions to be successful in the world, or we can choose to be in this world, but not of it.

Simply put, we can limit how much negativity we absorb in our lives by what we view, how we interact, what environments we participate in and how we choose our relationships.

We can choose to put ourselves in circumstances and experiences that are positive and enriching and not give our attention to the negative currents that distract our soul-based perspective.

It is our choice to see the negativity for what

it is – mind-based illusions that produce conflict, drama and pain – and avoid it. And once we recognize this distinction and minimize the negativity in our lives, we can invest our energy in what is positive and facilitates a soul-like state of being.

In other words, once we isolate the negative, we liberate the positive. And the positive facilitates the soul-like state of being where we can manifest our desires.

Another important component of manifestation is avoiding the "what if" traps: What if this doesn't happen; what if this does happen and it's not like I anticipated; what if I am desiring the wrong thing; what if my desires do not match, etc. "What if" scenarios are endless and each one is a distraction to our ability to manifest and shape our lives how we desire.

By nature, "what if" is a future construct, a scenario-based assumption that assesses risk and the likely effects of unanticipated variables.

This is an important analytical process in

math and science, but irrelevant to the process of manifesting desires.

Remember, desires emanate from the soul. They are an expression of energy and information that we are consciously bringing into our lives to enhance our circumstances and enrich our experiences.

They are not moves on a board or a step down a path; they are the embodiment of what will shape our lives in a positive and productive way.

Manifesting our desires is a soul-based process which energizes this moment in order to imbue the next one with meaning and potential.

There is no "what if" in the soul, only perfect process and meaningful development. No analysis is required and no future assessments are applicable.

We manifest what we desire in this moment and the desire manifests in our lives in the next. It is not the future that we are embracing in this process. It is this moment where all our potential for happiness and opportunity resides.

Finally, it is important to understand that, although we have focused on manifesting desires into our lives, we can equally manifest our wants with the same process of soul-based connectedness.

A want, as we discussed earlier, is a mind-based acquisition based on pleasure. It is transitory and most often focused on satisfying an appetite or enhancing a resource that will make us more successful.

There is nothing wrong with having wants as long as we know their distinction from desire, and there is nothing wrong with pleasure as long as we know its distinction from happiness.

A balanced life is lived in both the physical and spiritual world – through the mind and the soul – and both want and desire are integral to achieving success in their respective planes.

Thus, with an understanding of the distinction between want and desire, you can use the same concentration and focus to manifest your wants.

From the superficial to the sublime, the process works just as effectively for both your wants and desires. The only catch is that there is a hierarchy.

Desire always comes first and, if you are trying to manifest a want that conflicts or competes with a desire, you will not achieve your want. This is a good thing.

Remember, desire produces happiness and want produces pleasure. If you fulfill a desire, you have brought lasting contentment into your life.

If you achieve a want, you have brought transitory satisfaction into your life.

The goal is to understand this distinction and to maintain perspective when you don't manifest a want.

In fact, not achieving a want is a perfect opportunity to reconnect to your desires and assess what will manifest in your life that will be even better and lasting. It is a perfect opportunity to reaffirm your ability to shape your life the way you like and know that you are always the steward of your own happiness.

Let's look at an example. You really want a certain job that just came available. It fits your skills and talents perfectly. It is financially rewarding and an excellent step in your career progression. You love the organization and the people, and you know you'll be a perfect fit in the corporate culture and an important contributor to its mission.

You submit your application and, after several rounds of interviews, you make it to the final selection between you and another candidate.

You feel certain you have the job after your final interview and you are all but celebrating on the inside in anticipation of the offer.

But then you don't get the job.

How is that possible? All the ingredients were there for a perfect transition in your career.

There was the right money, the right skill set, the right fit and the right time for you. All the indicators throughout the process pointed towards your selection and you remained committed to this achievement to the very end.

There is no doubt in your mind you had manifested this job into your life; you wanted it for all the right reasons.

A few nights later, you're at a dinner party and

engaged in conversation with a friend about your professional dilemma.

You share all the points of symmetry you had found in this job opportunity and try to make sense of how this could have happened. Your friend is empathetic and supportive, but you still don't feel comforted.

There seems to be no meaning in your failure to get the job, and you begin to doubt your ability to manifest what you want in your life.

Your friend suggests you join him on a mini-vacation to a city in another state to get your mind off your predicament...and then it hits you.

The city that your friend suggests has been on your mind for several years as an ideal place to live. You have even gone as far as to research the lifestyle and opportunities in this location, but you have never visited.

You readily accept the offer and you make plans to travel there together that coming weekend. In the back of your mind all you can think is: "Is this what I have been desiring?"

You arrive in the city eager to get acquainted

with what's available there and your friend is a willing companion in exploring all that you want. You spend the weekend driving around the city visiting entertainment and recreational destinations, feeling more encouraged with every stop.

You are growing more excited with every venue you visit and, at your last destination, a coffee shop, you pick up the local newspaper and look through the employment opportunities. You're wild with excitement when you find numerous positions very similar in scope to the one you'd wanted back home. You take the paper home with you and make a commitment to start applying.

Two weeks later, you land a job in this new city, a job more lucrative and more integral to your career progression than the one you initially had wanted.

You are floored by the twist of events, but it immediately makes sense.

Had you been offered the job you wanted, you would not have realized your desire to relocate to this new city.

It is clear that your want was valid, but your

desire to be in this city supplanted this want with something more meaningful, enriching and long-term.

You are energized by the whole experience as you can now clearly affirm your ability to manifest your desires.

You understand perfectly now that your wants are just the backdrop on the stage that is your life, while your desires are the production. You are resolved to employ this perspective in everything you do in your life and to find true happiness in all your choices.

You know now that you are a participant in the living world and the director of your life.

You are spiritually endowed to shape your life exactly how you like and connected to all the energy and information that you need to create opportunities for success, happiness and inner-peace.

You finally feel truly connected and present.

The last chapter "Faith and Constitution" is about this perspective and the confidence to live within the realm of spiritual possibility.

You will find in the next chapter that the world around you has no bearing on who you are or who you will become, and that you have all the power and perspective you need inside to take control of your life and manifest your endless opportunities for success and happiness.

All you need are the faith and constitution to believe in the power of your soul, the meaning of your desires and the importance of your choices.

Do you have the strength to live in this world but flourish in another?

Do you have the courage to bring this other world into this one?

And do you have the fortitude to finally see your life through your soul, the portal into which all flows and flourishes and from which you draw all that will make you free.

CHAPTER 6

Faith and Constitution

EVEN IF THE PREVIOUS CHAPTERS have convinced you that you are a spiritual being with the innate capacity to live consciously and proactively in shaping your life according to your desires, the real challenge is maintaining your faith in this ability and the perspective to see through present circumstances to the destination, the manifestation of your desires.

We are programmed from an early age to view life as a series of challenges and opportunities that will define who we are and what we will do in this life.

We are conditioned to accept that sometimes life is just hard and things happen that are unfortunate.

We are taught that bad things happen to good people and sadness and frustration are natural components of a life regardless of how much we try.

Life is meant to be textured and rich with both good and bad experiences because that is what shapes us and develops our maturity and perspective.

We only live fully when we take the bad with the good.

But none of this is true.

These are mind-based perspectives on how life is supposed to unfold; they have nothing to do with how we can live and flourish in this world.

A life lived through the insight and perspective of the soul is free from all that is considered bad and unfortunate.

Through detachment and non-labeling, we can

accept our circumstances as a natural part of our evolution – the portal into the next moment which we have engineered to facilitate our desires.

But our mind, of course, tell us otherwise.

In fact, it screams it so loudly and so consistently that maintaining faith in our soul-based perspective sometimes seems impossible.

And our mind doesn't just tell us that this is bad or this is not what we wanted. It uses powerful emotions to convince us that what we are experiencing is not just real, but natural.

It convinces us that negative emotions are a natural part of our existence and, without them, we can't appreciate the positive ones.

This happens so convincingly and so consistently that we lose ourselves in the context our mind creates for us and accept it as our reality. And, ultimately, we lose faith in our ability to live a life beyond what the mind tells us to accept.

So, if we know the mind is using emotions to distract us from our soul-based perspective, we need to fully understand those emotions that are distracting us.

Among the dozens of emotions that we experience, there are four that cause the most disruption and discomfort in our lives. They are the four horsemen of the mind and the chief antagonists of the soul. They are the guardians of a fictitious future and the enemy of the present moment.

They are anxiety, frustration, panic and fear.

Anxiety is inhibition.

We feel constrained and limited in our capacity to commit to a desired action because we are worried about the potential outcome of a situation or circumstance.

We think more about what could go wrong than what could be achieved through action. We sit on the sidelines looking at the play that needs to be called but feel inhibited about participating in the action.

Anxiety traps us in a perpetual state of indecision and inaction and, ultimately, we either choose inaction or the wrong action because we are inhibited from seeing the outcome in a clear context.

We are confined to that limiting mental

perspective of "what if" and seek comfort in inaction to avoid the danger of an uncomfortable context that may be created through action.

An example. You want to attend a social function but have anxiety that you may not feel comfortable in that environment or may not know anybody to engage in conversation. You are anxious about participating in the gathering and choose not to attend to avoid discomfort and, more importantly, to suppress the feeling of anxiety.

Anxiety wins, opportunity loses.

Instead of visualizing a comfortable, fluid social opportunity and manifesting a desire to be engaged and engaging in an enjoyable situation, you allow the "what if" to control your actions and how you feel about it. You trap yourself in a worried state and allow your mind to create a reality that doesn't exist.

Anxiety obscures the soul-based perspective of opportunity and your faith in your ability to manifest circumstances you desire is shaken.

But the reality is you never gave faith a chance.

The "what if" of anxiety eclipsed your faith and

you lost both awareness and opportunity – awareness that you have the ability to manifest your circumstances and the opportunity to prove it.

Frustration is lost perspective.

We feel frustrated because we see a certain circumstance or situation in a way that it is not. When we are frustrated, it's because our mind is not satisfied that it has achieved success according to the recipe it created.

Our mind tells us that we have failed and to discard the situation as something we have no control over rather than engage it and feel discomfort.

But that is not what has happened at all.

If you feel frustrated, it's because you don't recognize the opportunity associated with a circumstance or situation that came into your life, an opportunity that will facilitate your choosing another path that will take you towards your true desire.

Just because you do not achieve what you projected does not mean you failed; that is a mind-based conclusion.

Your soul does not mine circumstances and situations for clues that you have achieved a goal; it only sees them for what they are – facilitators to the moment that you engineered for success.

You can use the simplest, everyday examples to see the fallacy of frustration: You are stuck in traffic; you are waiting too long in line; the store closes before you get there; you're trying to reach someone on the phone who's not responding...the list is endless.

But none of these situations imply failure.

They are just situations in which you did not achieve what your mind projected would be an ingredient in your success.

If you look just one degree beyond the frustrating situation, you'll see that it is always either a facilitator to a moment you truly desired or an opportunity to mine clues with respect to the desire you are manifesting.

In other words, if you remove the context of time and expectation, you'll clearly see that nothing comes into your life to impede you.

Shift your perspective from your mind to

your soul and you will restore your faith in the significance of every situation in your life and, more importantly, in your ability to manifest your desires.

Frustration is a choice, as is faith.

Panic is surrender.

Probably one of the worst negative emotions we experience, panic overrides every capacity we have to function and stay conscious in the present moment.

It is debilitating and disruptive to the point that all options for action seem to evaporate, leaving only a fog of confusion.

Panic is the most powerful weapon our mind has to impede our moving forward into the next moment, where our mind tells us we will risk certain destruction.

When we are panicking, we are surrendering to our mind. We become a willing audience to a series of pictures that our mind has created to prove to us that complete doom is near.

We risk everything we have and will ever

have if we engage that circumstance or situation that the mind has classified as code red. Surrender now or risk self destruction.

But the reality is panic is the ultimate smoke screen produced in your mind to obscure the courage and perspective that emanates from your soul.

If your mind is working in overdrive to convince you that danger lies beyond in that circumstance or situation, it is probably because that circumstance or situation is where you will transform yourself, your life and your destiny.

This is the moment where you will embrace the desire you have manifested, and your mind cannot allow that passage because it will change the ingredients for success your mind has created.

There is no change in the mind, just small course corrections that do not conflict with the overall picture of success it has projected.

Thus, that circumstance or situation that could be transforming is the enemy of the mind, and it will do everything it can to prevent you from approaching it.

My entrepreneurial pursuit contains the most lucid examples of panic that you can imagine. As I shared earlier, I launched my venture with the expectation that it would take six months to a year to get off the ground. I worked tirelessly towards that goal and, after a year, I was close, but still not there.

I invested more of my own resources to continue the process and took on more business debt to keep the momentum going.

As I approached the end of the second year, the projects still had momentum, but I still had not reached the finish line. I depleted what I had left and took on more debt because the projects were still very viable.

I continued to work diligently towards the successful conclusion of the venture and, as I approached the end of the third year, my descent into panic began. I had taken on a mountain of business debt to get these projects to the funding table, and I had completely depleted myself of all my resources and my ability to acquire more to keep the process moving.

Not only had the picture of my success changed, but now I was financially in trouble and sinking quickly into the worst possible scenario.

Panic was now a daily staple and my mind was working overtime to make me eject from the ship. From my mind's perspective, I was out of options and the ultimate danger was just around the corner. Surrender was the only path.

But, by this time in my business pursuit, I had learned the contrast between the mind and the soul and had ultimate faith in my ability to manifest my desires.

I addressed the panic with this faith and eliminated it. It returned periodically as the venture continued forward, but this same faith kept rendering it powerless in its attempts to force me to abandon my desire.

I had faith in my ability to manifest my desires, and I had the constitution, because of this faith, to endure the haunting pictures my mind kept sending me of what was certain destruction.

And, with the panic marginalized, my soul-based creativity returned and I managed to find the resources I needed to continue forward. The resources were always there, but the panic had obscured them.

My mind could not allow me to tap into this creativity because it wanted me to stop moving towards my desire. It was unsuccessful and, ultimately, powerless over my faith in my ability to manifest my desire.

Now, in the fourth year, the projects look nothing like I had originally visualized and financial peril is quickly turning into financial destruction, yet, I still remain undeterred.

My mind continues to send me pictures of very uncomfortable circumstances should I continue on this path, but I am no longer distracted by its attempts to force me to surrender.

As of this writing, I am on the proverbial financial cliff, but I remain committed to a desire I asked to manifest four years ago.

I remain faithful that I will be successful in some shape or form and that the transformation I will experience at the conclusion of this process will be both positive and instrumental to the manifestation of my next desire.

I have perfect faith in my ability to manifest the desires in my life, and the tools of the mind that help preserve its narrow vision of success are not going to dilute an ounce of that faith.

Panic is a choice. Faith is a commitment...a commitment to myself and an expression of gratitude to my soul.

Finally, fear is paralysis.

Unlike the inhibition of anxiety or the surrender of panic, the paralysis of fear still involves action, but with an overly cautious, skewed interpretation of the results of that action.

It's a tainted perspective on what could go wrong if an action is pursued, which renders the resulting action either ineffective or inaccurate.

The mind uses fear to direct us in a way so as to minimize the risks and potential disruption to its view of success.

When we are fearful, we feel vulnerable to potentially negative outcomes, and we choose actions that will keep us safe but still productive and moving towards the narrow vision of success that emanates from the mind.

We accept the pictures of danger from our mind and we feel enveloped in doom as we move down a path that will minimize risk yet still supposedly yield results.

But this overly cautious action of minimizing risk conflicts with the proper action that will manifest our desires. We are in the ballpark but not playing our position.

The creativity and perspective of the soul is eclipsed, so, although we are moving forward, we are not truly mining the potential of that path. The result is partial success and, ultimately, personal dissatisfaction with the outcome of that success.

We manifest only a fraction of our desire in this process of fear, and the resulting dissatisfaction of not achieving our full desire weakens our faith in our ability to manifest the next one.

Here's an example of fear and the dissatisfaction it causes in our lives.

You desire to change jobs, but you are scared

that if you leave your present employment you will not find the same salary and opportunity that you have in your current position. You do take some action and apply for other positions, and you are somewhat diligent in your efforts to make a professional move, but you move cautiously, only looking at those positions that are very comparable to what you have right now.

While you are taking steps towards this professional move, you are asked to apply for a new position within your current firm and you eventually get this new assignment. It involves more pay and more responsibility, and you're initially satisfied you have found a better professional situation and, thus, stop looking for other opportunities.

Six months later, you are just as dissatisfied as you were when you began looking for another opportunity.

You achieved a partial desire to change jobs, but you did not realize the full potential of your desire to find a new job because you were overly cautious in your approach to finding one you would truly enjoy.

You had fear that any professional transition you made that was not very similar to your present situation would involve too much risk and, thus, you did not pursue other positions that could have yielded more satisfaction.

You did not have faith in your ability to fully manifest your desire to make a change professionally, so you accepted a partial fulfillment in more pay and responsibility.

Your mind was successful in getting you to make a small course correction instead of a change, and you feel unsuccessful in manifesting your true desire.

Fear paralyzed you and your faith in your ability to manifest your desires is now weakened.

Fear wins. Faith loses.

The opportunity to live a life based on our ability to manifest our desires lies within the elimination of anxiety, frustration, panic and fear.

We cannot accept the inhibition of anxiety, the perspective loss of frustration, the surrender of panic and the paralysis of fear and still exist within the insight, understanding, wisdom and perspective of the soul.

We cannot connect to our soul portal through which we access all the energy and information of the living world if we succumb to the mind and stay on the shore, far from the sea of opportunity, creativity and happiness.

We have to sail the waters of spiritual connectedness if we are going to manifest a life we truly desire.

Living consciously and purposefully in the pursuit of our desires is a choice.

Having faith in our ability to manifest our desires is a choice.

Having the personal constitution to live a life fully and richly is a choice.

And knowing that all the possibilities for success and happiness lie within us is a gift we give ourselves.

My hope is that you will give this gift to yourself.

CHAPTER 7

Perspective Checklist

THE LIST ON THE FOLLOWING PAGES is a reminder checklist to refer to when the constraint of your mind begins to eclipse the opportunity of your soul.

It is a compilation of all the themes and concepts introduced in the previous chapters.

Use it to stay focused on your desires and connected to the endless possibilities that you can manifest in your life.

Remember, the feeling of failure has no bearing on what you are capable of achieving, and the feeling of fear has no relevance to the opportunity of the present moment.

What may seem overwhelming right now is a construct of the mind and a product of time. The true path that is taking you to your desires can never be compromised by either.

Now that you know the difference between soul-based perspective and mind-based perception, you can always disassociate yourself from a feeling that attempts to compromise the truth... that you are in control of your life and the process of shaping your life how you desire is perfect.

Happiness resides in this truth. It's up to you to embrace it.

1. Your mind is just a tool you use to navigate the physical world.

2. The painful thoughts and feelings you experience are just mind-based perceptions of a situation or circumstance that has no impact on who you are or will become. Allow your mind to generate its thoughts and feelings without censure. Just know that you are not defined by any of it.

3. Your soul exists outside of you and is your connection to all the energy and information and, thus, opportunity, in the living world.

4. All the insight, understanding, wisdom and perspective you need to shape your life how you desire emanates from the soul.

5. There is nothing you or your mind can do to impair your soul and its infinite possibilities.

6. Whether through prayer, meditation or focus, you are always tapped into the same source of unlimited potential and creativity of the soul.

7. Never disregard any information or "hint" you may receive in your life. Everything has relevance if mined for the clues you are looking for to confirm your desired path.

8. Desires are rooted in the soul; wants are generated in the mind. Both are valid as long as you know the distinction and the value of each in your life.

9. Always live detached from the mind-based perception of success. Live fully in this world but appreciate the impact of your actions in the other – the opportunity and creativity your efforts generate for the rest of the living world.

10. There is no such thing as failure. It is only a non-achievement of something that your mind projected as attainable. You never fail in your true desires.

11. Live free from the approval of others. Don't rebel or disassociate from the world, but live your life and manifest your desires according to your will, not that of society.

12. Don't apply the labels of good and bad to the circumstances and situations in your life. Every moment has value in the achievement of your desires, even if you can't see it clearly at the time.

13. Your personal power is a choice. Live with insight and self-awareness and you will always have the resources you need for personal development and growth.

14. If you feel like you are losing control to your mind in the pursuit of your desires, do a past inventory of the previous day, week or month. Take note of how you accomplished all that you needed to continue your momentum on your path.

15. Remember the distinction between evolutionary and achievement desires – the first is personal growth and the second is accomplishment of a goal. Both can coexist and complement each other as they manifest in your life.

16. Be conscious that you always have your soul available to you to deposit a desire. If you are anxious or fearful in a situation, turn your worry into a wish and allow your soul to do the rest. Your acknowledgement of this portal into the energy and information of the living world is all you need to begin the process of manifesting your desires.

17. Always be positive – it marginalizes your mind and connects you to your soul.

18. There are no "what ifs" in the manifestation of your desires. Don't analyze the validity or probability of what you desire in your life – just draw those desires to you without qualification.

19. You are engineering every moment in your life. Have faith that your soul is guiding you to your desires. No anxiety, no frustration, no panic and no fear.

20. Live consciously and know that no negative, mind-based scenario or emotion can deter you from your path and your desires. Your personal power is more powerful than your mind, and, if you have faith in this power, you have faith in your desires. Allow both to flourish.

NOTES

NOTES

NOTES

NOTES

NOTES

NOTES

NOTES

NOTES

NOTES

NOTES

NOTES